STEPS IN AVOIDING SEX FOR TEENS AND YOUTH

BRO EMMANUEL NWACHUKWU

Contents

- The language of sex
- The Dichotomy of sex
- Understanding sex in the body of teens and all youth
- Teachings on how to stay pure

Preface

it is all struggle that we all have experienced in one way or the other. Some have overcome, others are yet to while others won't.

It is a struggle of the human mind not necessarily the emotions. The power is within us though we do not realize it to do and not do what we want. How to come to terms with that power, this book would show you.

THE
Language
Of

SEX

WHAT IS SEX?

It is the act of sensual intercourse whereby a man and a woman bond together in human ways.

This definition is the most academic definitions on sex. You can look at it scientifically, religiously or chemically those are just views and there are no conducting of experiments during sex neither is it a philosophical thing, it's just human.

It is human and physical to have sex just that the human type carries out a bonding beyond the physical horizon by means of all that God has put in to facilitate His agenda and purpose of it.

Now we want to understand the language of sex, not religiously, not academically neither by means of variant opinions of the less scholarly on the subject. If humans can understand there environment I bet they purposefully utilize same environment.

I would be using texts from the bible why? I guess it is to most suitable for many reasons. One reason is that it captures it in the ways unimaginably for supposedly holy texts. Most religious books identify rituals tend to hide facts but the bible if you be a keen reader might discover unimaginable ways of this bonding. The bible is a testament of all God has created, all that he has done upon this earth. You can call a book about the deeds of God, especially if you believe in God and a one God theology I believe unbiasedly that you would find the bible a reasonable required text to know about God. The Hebrews you use it, it is the foundation for the Quran texts and largely have influenced the academic world. The most basic book about the study of God and religion, thoroughly a great work of arts.

Sex outside the religious phase, is very intriguing, satisfying and unimaginably pleasant described by the bible as *…waters* and *… running waters…* think about what water means to a man from the east as of that time and you would understand what was in the mind of the writer.

Actually sex refreshes the body biologically, reduces body load and enhances the body security pathologically no wonder the Hebrew text advises us to DRINK… so it is good for us to DRINK…

WHAT WE LEARN FROM THE BIBLE ABOUT SEX?

Like I said I would be allowed to use my freedom to refer to what sex is using the bible. We would be separating sex from the bible's moral code, many celibacy advocating preachers throughout history using the old texts have mumbled both together- sex and the moral code for sex.

Sex in terms of the ancient men was a place of refuge. Usually the old kjv translations uses the word KNOW, meaning it was a way of knowing your wife. Who would not want to know his wife better?

Sex as it is put is a purifier, it helps to avert sexual impurities. This means that the way of preventing sex is by having sex, ironic isn't? Yeah! This is where the moral code comes in. You had to have a wife at least compared to today by 18 years yes! Both female and male! In ancient times it was far less maybe fifteen or sixteen.

HOW THE BIBLE SPOKE OF SEX?

Proverbs 5:15-21   proverbs 6:6, 30-32.

The moral code is included, the physical understanding is related.

It is an advice for men and boys alike. You should endeavor to drink, have sex but with a woman who is to be your wife. It means that the woman has been legally married to you. It is important to state that you are in no way equipped whether spiritually or physically to overpower the yearnings of sex. You can fast it, control it, refuse do it but you can never stop it-it is God given.

It metaphorically instructs that this fountain MUST be dispersed abroad. It is deep to explain this but you must know how to make well your wife, she is your own enjoy her. She is to be a blessing by your side but she must categorically and uniquely be thy own not another person with you. This nullifies dating where you are in relationship with several partners trying to find the best. You can be in a non commitant relationship but you have to stay away from sex with all of them.

It says rejoice-be happy with the wife of thy youth/boyhood. It shows boys can court till they are ready for marriage only that no sex be allowed in that relationship in whichever form. As of eighteen you should be fully aware who you should marry. From twenty one if the devil is not on your trail, you should get married. Some for which ever reason can stay till thirty but whatever purpose human caused delay should not make you marry after forty that is the deadline. That is marriage as understood in the bible.

Sex should be done sweetly, yes how? Make her the loving hind… and pleasant roe… of your life. This are almost the same only in intensity it differs both are not similar and alike though. A hind and a roe is different but they are deer. She has to be a deer-a loving/intoxicating/sweeting and a pleasant, tenderly cared for young deer. This enjoyment goes to the way of fun and satisfaction. Now you might request to know how her breast can satisfy you, I will would tell you. Ezekiel 23:7, 8, 10, 18-21. The bible is filled with this elaborateness because if you are truly obedient to the word you won't know this except the word shows you.

The bible also talks about this in other ways, the lovers book of the Song of Solomon is quite educating on this aspect. If you would know how to express love keenly read it but now every youth should balance this up-love and wisdom the reason for the Song of Solomon and the book of proverbs. It is good to love and enjoy sex but the balance is this- with the one you have married, the one who you would legally be enjoying doing this with.

Marriage depends on the culture of the people you want to marry and you must be peaceful about. What is principal here is her Father, he is the one to give consent to it Exodus 22:14-17. Marriage is legally taken possession of once daughter so it had to involve bride price/dowry. Some cultures have some traditions and customs that are to be done away with especially as regarding marriage. Today as it is seen in biblical text , Jesus the perfection has come. The perfection of the law is Jesus because as it is written …all prophets and the law prophesied till john… so now effectively by that statement by Jesus a new dispensation has begun and now certain rules have to be updated with the status quo. Bride price or dowry is not as effective as of when the days of old began, things have changed. Today here is the change 1 Corinth 7:6-11, 12-15. The main emphasis is if two people are interested in marrying each other no hindrances [even dowry] should be put in their way. The command is LET THEM MARRY. Yes or No is the answer of purity anything after that the savior says it is from the evil one. Now here the bible said you have to say YES, which means the third party should not come in between them if they have decided except once they are not in agreement, it primarily rests on them to decide. Man and woman has to agree even if they are not believers in the same thing no priest or religious figure should decide only they. You can advise but you should not control.

Dear if you have decided to marry him, if you have decided to marry her please go on, let no one stop you and do it fast except for any reason higher.

THE DICHOTOMY OF SEX

We have seen the diverse variances in sex and as well as the commandments in sex. We have captured the essentials cunningly under the term the Language of sex. If you do not understand it's language you cannot speak it's language and it would remain a stranger to you.

The dichotomy of sexual relationship-the relationship involving sex is into two products. The first product is PLEASURE and CHILD DELIVERY and reproduction. In the pleasure you have the humanics but in reproduction you have the biology. Humanics which I guess should be a future study should largely be about the study of the invisible unionizing of the specie called man. Not social unity, not political, religious, philosophical nor idealogical but something close to spiritual, abstract, invisible hidden not objectively obvious at all. I guess 99% of humans know nothing of the sphere of humanics. It is the ability of humans to study themselves intricately, so the in-depth study of human to human and the deep things with it. I defined it this way for a lack of a better way of defining it.

I LEAVE THIS TOPIC
AND I SAY TO
HUMANS THINK...

UNDERSTANDING SEX IN THE BODY OF TEENS AND ALL YOUTH

I am not striving to inform you about what is you already know but about what you do not know. What you do not know is far bigger, better and larger than what you do not know.

Biologically sex is a thriving force, I guess youths should better best know their sexual possibilities with caution. Know yourself in all areas. It is an energy, an ability and a launching power, you combat, mix and arrange diversity by sex. It is a flow of power from the ancient to the know, I am a pyschelogist and I try to venture into the abstractedness as I study hidden knowledge about science itself, abstractedness of space, and the TRIPILE-DIPPLE dimension of matter, I would show you an example. The relationship between matter and volume.

Matter =m mass, kg

$V=1/3^3=1/3$

Every human being, animal or whatever occupies matter and volume. Here is the mathematical equation to support it.

M =kV which is first matter must be describe as a direct proportion and multiple of volume.

K is the determining factor if the relationship must be defined. In itself k is constant but variably different comparing the quantities measured and in other words what might be k here cannot effectively be a k there.

Now little physics comes to play,

F=ma so

Kg.sec=kg.sec

But v=L*L*L so l^3.

We have M=k l^3

The psychelogy is now to understand the variation of the k. I to God's grace am the first person linking this body of knowledge together and calling it pyschelogy. Pyschelogy is the study of abstractedness, intrinsic nature not merely limited to space, time and length. It goes beyond force and energy or motion. It is a study on the SYSTEMS that makes things work and not merely the observable equation/evaluations. It seeks to pry into what are the *all* involve in this mechanism, how can it work in the way it is working and many more such questions. It doesn't dismiss reality as seen in other forms of knowledge but sees it as a distant truth conveyed to man through the vehicle of the MIND. It seeks to understand the interworkings of the mind and it's relationship with space and any hidden world. It is a study of systems!

I have written several works on this that would be highly beneficial to understanding my researches on pyschelogy, if you are interested in knowing.

For now this is readable only online.

Some pyschelogy principles are documented in this book.

The life of a youth is strong vibrant and deep. It would take a deepening study to release the fountain of your youth. Life is a measurement of what you can know as of in this plane.

The body of a youth healthily is a force, no wonder the book of psalms in the bible calls it an ARROW, it moves with great force depending on how it is short and how it is struck so comes my principle of the formidable youth.

Theory of the formidable youth

This is a youth strong, healthy, and persuasive.

A youth strong is a youth knowledgeable, mindful and thoughtful eating the right kind of food **both** for the body and for the mind. The body must be feed with the right kind of food and the mind must assimilate the right kind of knowledge.

Now he is skillful which means he has been trained.

He is armful- knows the right kind of weapon to use

Healthy youths both in mind and in soul and in body. They bear no deformity mostly in their minds and independent in their thoughts seeking knowledge *from where* it is found. They have maintained connection with their predecessors and haven't lost much wealth of knowledge from the past generation. Any that have wounds in this area is deficient cannot sustain what it takes to be strong and decisive. He is not a slave in his mind.it is only then by the factor of time that you would prove your element for persuasiveness as you would show your decisiveness.

. Teachings on how to stay pure

This is my last contribution to this matter. I would be speaking to Christians who I am drawing wisdom from their texts. Every Christian must realize something, the bible you hold speaks a lot about sex because it is human to be sexual and angelic to be celibate. If you are not a sexual being you are either defaulted or angelic meaning having the bodies of angels. Or better still you are deceiving yourself, but I know that truly some people have crossed to the other side of not being human then you can safely say they are devils. For as far as you can fertilize a woman then you are a man. No man is incapable of being taken over by the feelings of sex because it is our strength not our weakness. What actually is our weakness is the inability of controlling ourselves, the bible blames the event of Eden, the fruit [it is believed to be sex with the serpent by some scholars] introduce the faultiness that we have among us today. Naturally we should be able to know when to have sex and when not to and not to be wicked about it or either given over to it. To solve that the bible records that God sent His Son [identified in spirit sense as His word] to make it possible for God to do it by dying on man's behalf because God would not forgive man if he doesn't die and man since then still dies only that Jesus said that if you believe in Him then you have the hope of resurrection. Now the correction of that anomaly of the Edenic event is called BORN AGAIN in biblical literature. Here it is believed that you must repent, believe on Jesus, get baptized in water and ask in faith for God's Spirit who would come and perform that miracle for you. Many different people ever since have affirmed that they have been born again and there seems to be compelling evidences scholarly to say evidently that can be true. Meanwhile a truth about anything is known about what it testifies about itself. The bible says that the body of knowledge it has is secretive and only a group of people [spiritual men] can really decipher it's truths. It best bet that if you want to know search for them they should be in the best custody of knowledge apart from that you can probably pray to God if you believe that He exist (I myself do) that He should better reveal to you or you can safely depend on the text (the Bible) to find your way through. Lastly I want to say that I have made many mistake, alas committed many sins, including areas relating to impurities as of this topic I am referring to in this chapter and even as a Christian, my only guess is that I believe God would forgive as it is affirmed for sinners in the Bible.\

Other books authored by the same author.

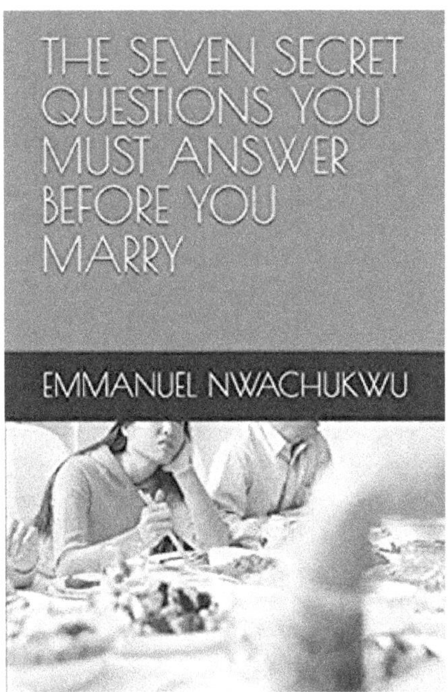

EMMANUEL
NWACHUKWU
THE
SEX -
ADDICT

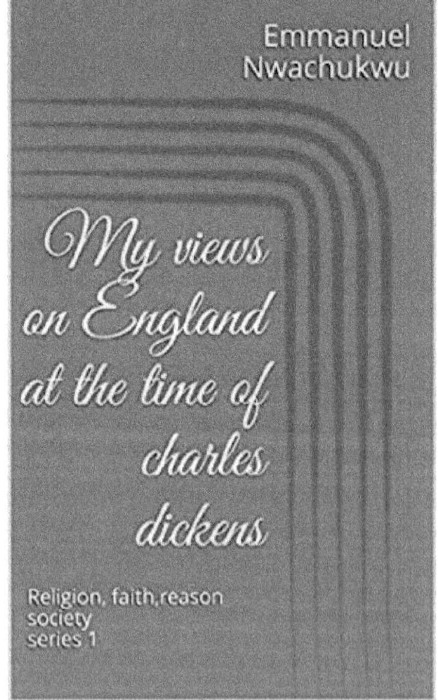

Emmanuel
Nwachukwu
My views
on England
at the time of
charles
dickens
Religion, faith, reason
society
series 1

BABYLON, THE FALSE PROPHET, THE BEAST AND THE DRAGON
(A scriptural investigation, an unveiling of the scriptural prediction of the End-times)
EMMANUEL NWACHUKWU

PLOT YOUR TAKE-OVER
EMMANUEL NWACHUKWU

Want to know more about the Author?

Write a mail to Emmanuel Nwachukwu

+2349029043621, enwachukwu127@gmail.com

Thank you!

www.ingramcontent.com/pod-product-compliance
Lightning Source LLC
Chambersburg PA
CBHW052339150726

47998CB00018B/2644